Nurturing Positive Behaviors In Your Classroom

Lynn Staley

Illustrations by Lori Ricciardi Wright

First Edition © 2009 Lynn Staley

Published by First Steps Library
www.firststepslibrary.com

"It's You I Like" lyrics copyright © 1971 by Fred Rogers. Used by permission of Family Communications, Inc.

Printed in the United States of America
ISBN: 978-0-578-03763-9

AUTHOR CONTACT
Dr. Lynn Staley, Professor
Elementary Education TC 216
Ball State University
Muncie, IN 47306
765-285-8568
lstaley@bsu.edu

PUBLISHER CONTACT
First Steps Library
Flagship Enterprise Center
2701 Enterprise Drive
Box No. 213
Anderson IN, 46013

DESIGN AND LAYOUT
Community Networks
www.CommunityNet.biz

ILLUSTRATOR CONTACT
Lori Ricciardi Wright
lawright2@bsu.edu

Contents

Appreciation   iii

Dedication   v

INTRODUCTION   vii

CHAPTER ONE   1
Positive Child Guidance   1
    Developmentally Appropriate Guidance   3
    Developmentally Appropriate Curriculum   5

CHAPTER TWO   9
Self-Fulfilling Prophecy   9
    IALAC: I am Lovable and Capable   11

CHAPTER THREE   13
    Affirmation   14
    Attention   16
    Acceptance   19
    Affection   22
    Appreciation   23

CHAPTER FOUR   25
    Observation   25
       Of the whole child   26
       Of personality and temperament   28
    Documentation   30
    Reflection   32

CHAPTER FIVE   35
    Communication   35
       with "I Messages"   35
       with positive nonverbal language   38

with positive directions   38
with clear and specific instructions   40
with active listening   41
with appropriate choices   43
without asking "Why?"   43
with firmness and calmness   44
with professionalism   47

CHAPTER SIX   49
  Consistency   49
    by planning for transitions   50
    by maintaining appropriate rules, expectations   51
    by making "NO" mean "NO"   53
    by teaching children to listen   54
    by picking our battles   55
    by using natural and logical consequences   56
    by giving consistent feedback   57

CHAPTER SEVEN   59
  The Bigger Picture   59
    in the context of families   59
    in the context of health and wellness   61

CHAPTER EIGHT   65
  A Caring Community   65
    within the classroom   65
    within the school   68
  Our Best Advice   69

References   71
Additional Resources   77
Children's Literature   83
Praise from Pre-Service Teachers   87
About the Author   89
About the First Steps Library   91

Appreciation

I am indebted to the many teachers who willingly shared their stories to assist others as they create caring communities in their classrooms. While we have chosen not to identify them by name to protect the identity of their schools, their children, and their families, please know that they are truly teachers of excellence. As they walk through the doors of their classrooms every morning, they "walk on stage." They know their children will be watching them closely. They are the "stars of the show." Their children adore them and will never forget them. I am truly blessed to know these educators and proud to consider them my friends and colleagues.

DEDICATION

This book is dedicated to my family.

My husband is my biggest fan and always supports my new ideas.

My son was the oldest of our two children, so I made lots of mistakes as a Mom, but he never seemed to mind; he loved me anyway. He was killed in an accident at age 13, and I miss the way he made us all laugh.

My daughter always encourages me to press on, even when I am weary of the obstacles that always accompany a new project. As a future teacher herself, she was my best critic. If something wasn't clear to her, I knew you would be confused, too. This book has become "notes to my daughter" - everything she needs to know about working with children in positive ways that I didn't want to forget to tell her.

INTRODUCTION

The *First Steps* focuses on children from PK-6 and is intended for those of you who are looking forward to a new career in education, as well as those of you who are experienced teachers and just want to be reminded of what you already know. We don't profess to have all the answers here; no one does. There are no recipes when working with children; there are no magic formulas or "one-size-fits-all" answers. There are, however, some fundamental and foundational strategies that benefit all children and often *prevent* difficulties.

What follows are the *First Steps* for your life long journey as a "guidance professional" (Gartrell 2001). These are the foundational strategies used by excellent teachers. You might think of this as a "zoom-out" map on the internet. We will talk only about the fundamentals – the basics or the "big" picture; you will need to "zoom-in" later for more detail on specific issues (i.e., special needs, aggression, biting, and bullying). Along the way, you will surely face hurdles, obstacles, difficulties, and frustrations. You will find a solution that works today but fails tomorrow. Strategies that are successful with one child may fail with another. This is not a book of solutions for all classroom problems; there is no such book. These *First Steps*, however, are absolutely essential if you are to establish caring, respectful, and positive relationships with your children.

CHAPTER ONE

"We never make kids do better by making them feel worse."
- Bev Boss

Positive Child Guidance

What is positive child guidance? Is it the same thing as discipline? The word discipline actually means to teach (Merriam-Webster 1989); it is synonymous with instruction. However, when we ask parents and non-educators to define discipline, the answer is always the same: "Discipline means punishment." Punishment promotes fear and shame and is often negative, threatening, blaming, humiliating, nagging, criticizing, embarrassing, and, in some cases, abusive. What do children learn from punishment? What do elementary children learn from losing recess? It rarely produces long-term change.

A university supervisor observed numerous fourth and fifth graders sitting in the hall every morning. What does the public rejection, embarrassment, and humiliation of sitting out in the hall teach children? Why should any child be removed from teaching and learning? When Readdick and Chapman (2000) interviewed 42 young children following time-out, they reported that most of the children expressed feeling "alone, disliked by one's teacher, and ignored by one's peers, as well as feelings of sadness and fear" (81). Furthermore, the children were unable to recall why they were in time-out, which reduced the likelihood of changed behavior. Rather than more time-out, perhaps children need more "time-in" with YOU to learn more effective strategies than the "act first, think later" used by most children.

Considering many common misconceptions about the term "discipline" and a focus on punishment, *we prefer the term "child guidance," with a focus on teaching and learning.*

Do you want your children to learn responsibility?
Then give them opportunities to be helpful.

Do you want them to learn how to get along with others?
Then teach them social skills and how to resolve conflicts.

Do you want them to learn respect for others?
Then engage them in cooperative learning activities.

Do you want them to learn independence?
Then give them reasonable choices so they experience the satisfaction of making competent decisions.

Do you want them to learn self-control?
Then teach them to wait and be patient with others.

If our goal is to teach children responsibility, social skills, independence, and self-control, it won't happen when children are punished. (The remaining chapters will elaborate on effective classroom strategies to promote the above.)

Developmentally Appropriate Guidance

Positive child guidance is developmentally appropriate for the group that you teach; it is "age appropriate, individually appropriate, and culturally appropriate" (Copple & Bredekamp 2006, 14). Our expectations and interventions are appropriate for the age group. We know that effective guidance strategies for five-year-olds will not work with fifth graders. We would not expect kindergartners to sit quietly and listen to a story for 30 minutes; their subsequent inattention would not be an issue of misbehavior but rather inappropriate expectations of the adult; choose a shorter and more appropriate book. It is the teacher's responsibility to know the developmental characteristics of the children in the class. A teacher quit using timed math drills because she was more interested in the children knowing the facts rather than "beating the clock." An example of what NOT to do: When walking down the hall, second graders were required to hold onto a knotted rope (such as those used with toddlers). When the children were observed crying and screaming down the hall, embarrassed and unable to please this excessively strict teacher, the teacher yelled, "I TOLD YOU TO BE STILL RIGHT THIS MINUTE!" The principal stepped out of his office and sent her home for the rest of the day.

Individually, what is appropriate for Billy may not be appropriate for Sally. Scamardella and Daggett (1997) teach their children that "everyone has different needs and that in order to be treated fairly, we all need to be treated differently" (p. 8). Guiding children individually is usually more effective than trying to address the whole group. A child with ADHD, for instance, might be allowed to get out of his seat at timed intervals (using an hourglass), as long as he focuses

3

on his seat work. A child with special needs might sit next to the teacher's desk where she doesn't distract others. A child who disturbs others might be given a stress ball to help him pay attention to the lesson. It is the teacher's responsibility to really know each child, so you must observe very carefully.

Culturally, what is appropriate for Juan (Hispanic) may not be appropriate for Pierre (French). Do you know that a Native American child may not look you in the eye because it is culturally disrespectful? It is the teacher's responsibility to be familiar with the cultures repre-

4

sented in your classroom so that you promote respect for all families.

DEVELOPMENTALLY APPROPRIATE CURRICULUM

A wise teacher once said, "the curriculum is everything that happens in your classroom all day long" (Williams, 1998). What does it feel like to be a child in your class all day long, day after day? *A developmentally appropriate curriculum engages children in meaningful learning.* It is based on authentic assessment and observation; it matches children's learning needs. Classroom experiences which foster children's inquiry and exploration through multisensory, hands-on, and "minds-on" involvement help children grasp new concepts (Copple & Bredekamp 2006, p. 15). Incorporate technology and make learning exciting.

Children also co-construct their understanding of math, science, and social studies when they work cooperatively with others. When children are permitted to talk and search for answers together, they teach each other. Carefully structure group projects and teach children how to work with others; these are important life skills.

Observe closely when teaching: who understood the lesson? Who looked confused, uninterested, distracted? Misbehavior is often the symptom of a curriculum that is either too easy or too hard for individual students; it is a mismatch. A university supervisor observed two fifth graders intentionally misbehave every morning during math in order to be sent to the hall to escape a boring and unsuccessful experience.

Susan Humphrey (1989), a former kindergarten teacher, also discovered the role of a developmentally appropriate curriculum:

> I used to be like that teacher who showed the [children] how to do everything. . . . I ran a completely teacher-directed program. . . . The classroom was mine and not theirs. . . . I did

not see problems as learning experiences for the children, but rather as challenges for me to solve. . . . I valued compliance more than cooperation. . . . The first year was really hard. In theory, I really wanted to give the children more responsibility and fewer constraints, but in reality it made me very nervous and uncomfortable. . . . I used to think of ways that I could help that problem child fit into our program. Now when a problem comes up, the first thing I consider is whether that problem is the child's or mine. Does the child need to change or do I need to adjust the program to make it more flexible and appropriate for that particular child so that he or she can feel successful? Because young children usually feel "I am what I can do," it's probably more important . . . to find out and emphasize what the children can do, not what they can't do. . . . My classroom is in the process of becoming more child-centered (17-20).

Is your curriculum boring, frustrating, and tedious? Or is it challenging and engaging? A kindergarten teacher reserved an entire day in the spring for her children to create Space Adventures. She creatively integrated literacy, numeracy, and science standards, as the children built space stations to accompany their adventure stories. As the children worked in small groups, she also taught them how to negotiate and compromise with others. She also made documentation boards (photos accompanied by the children's quotes) to record this exciting day. Believe it or not, some of the final stories were nine pages long, written by kindergartners!

Another kindergarten teacher wanted to ignite her children's interest in her science lesson about the human body. She told the children Professor Perriwinkle (posing as Bill Nye the science guy) was coming today. The teacher then exited the room and quickly donned her lab coat and stethoscope to re-enter as Professor Perriwinkle.

Making sure that your curriculum is developmentally appropriate is the very First Step of Positive Child Guidance.

CHAPTER TWO

"Children will be what you already say they are."
- Lillian Katz

SELF-FULFILLING PROPHECY

What do you believe about your children? What do you *really* believe? If you believe they are wonderful and special, they will be. If on the other hand, you believe they are a constant source of frustration, they will be exactly that. Children depend upon your reflection of them; you are their mirror. They can't see themselves without you. They develop their personal identity from who you say they are. ***Expect the best in your children and you will get it.*** Eliza Doolittle, in *My Fair Lady*, said, "The difference between a flower girl and a lady is not how she behaves but how she is treated!" How do you treat your children? Do they know that you truly believe the best in them? "What you think of me, I will think of me. What you think of me, I will be" (Bakley 1997).

A mother wanted her son, David (age 4), and her daughter, Catherine (age 2), to be close. She was an older parent and wanted the as-surance of knowing that no matter what happened in later years, the children would be there for each other. When they were very young she taught them a special "thumbs together" sign at which time they would say "Best Buddies!" No one could do this special signal but David and Catherine. They assumed very early that they were "Best

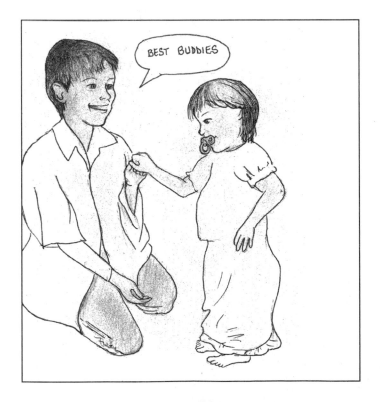

Buddies" because they said it was so and they just believed it. As they grew older, they did indeed have a very tender relationship. David was very protective of his little sister and Catherine's best friend in the whole world was her older brother. They were truly "Best Buddies" forever.

IALAC: I Am Lovable and Capable

Sydney Simon (1991) created a compelling story to remind us that all children are indeed lovable and capable. Every child, according to Simon, carries an invisible sign that says "IALAC," which means I Am Lovable and Capable. This sign reflects positive feelings of self. Every time a child receives a kind word or deed that boosts self-esteem, the sign magically twinkles and shines with a new brilliance. However, this same sign quickly becomes torn and stained when hurtful things are said. "What kind of stupid question is that?" "How many times do I have to tell you?" "You don't do anything right!" When teachers are condescending and inconsiderate, children lose respect and trust. When teachers nag and continually find fault, children quickly tune us out; they quit listening; they quit trying. It doesn't take long before the IALAC sign completely disappears and there is no hope for ever experiencing success. "The system works for everybody but me." "I can't win; why try?" "I never do anything right." " I don't fit in here." "The teacher never listens to me."

The good news, though, is that tender loving adults can restore the disappearing IALAC sign with affirmation, attention, acceptance, affection, and appreciation. "I want you to be all that you were meant to be." "You are my smartest class ever!" (Hint: Every class is the smartest class!) "I am going to call you my 'Smarties.'" "I will never let you do less than your best." "I am so proud of you." What do you see in your children? What do their IALAC signs look like? Do they wear IALAC over their heart or an "L" (for Loser) on their forehead? Do you forgive and forget their misbehaviors of today so that tomorrow their IALAC begins fresh and new? It is up to you.

How does it sound when you call their names? Tender, gentle, and affirming? Or harsh, loud, and condescending? How do you feel when your best friend or spouse says your name? Loved and valued?

Compare that to how you feel if the State Police stops you on the Interstate and says your name. Our names are a delicate component of who we are. When a teacher yells a child's name all day long, it only serves to whittle him down in his own sense of self, as well as in the eyes of his peers. When we speak every child's name with kindness and respect, it is the truest demonstration of our sincerity.

CHAPTER THREE

The Five A's of the heart keep a child feeling smart.

All children have five core needs in common: affirmation, attention, acceptance, affection, and appreciation (Linda Albert cited in Charles, 2005, p. 206). We call them the Five A's. When these needs are met and all children are taught to "consider and contribute to each other's well-being and learning" (Bredekamp & Copple 1997, 16), a caring community will emerge. While children don't always act in ways we like, believe it or not, their sincerest desire is to please us. "They [my kindergartners] come in [every morning] excited to see you and love you with all their heart, trying to please you" (a kindergarten teacher).

When discipline is seen as teaching and conveyed with a great deal of empathy and nurturing care, children feel good when they comply. It is a warm, nourishing feeling to feel that you are the gleam in someone else's eye. When the child is disappointed, he feels a sense of loss because he misses the positive regard that he has received when he has behaved appropriately. If he never had those positive feelings, there would be no sense of loss or disappointment to motivate him *from the inside* to change his behavior. . . Children [then] internalize standards when they feel nurtured, cared for by others and respected. When such a system is in place and children are guided by inner values, they make wise judgments about their behavior, because they are pleasing not just their parents or their teachers, but they are pleasing their own inner sense of self (Brazelton & Greenspan 2000, 146-147).

AFFIRMATION

There are no "bad kids." All children are worthy of our affirmation, regardless of their behavior. We separate who they are from what they do. We all make mistakes; the trick is to learn from those mistakes. Are they problem children or children who simply have problems that require your guidance and intervention? While their misbehaviors may be unacceptable, our children always know that we care about them. There are no strings attached; they don't have to earn our love; we love them unconditionally and consistently.

We focus our attention on children's strengths rather than on everything they do wrong. (Portfolios are a great way of documenting successes.) Are they precious or pests? Are they clever or clumsy? Are they stupendous or stupid? Are they happy or helpless? Think of a magnifying glass. Look very carefully to see the beautiful hidden qualities that each child possesses. The one who can't sit still and keep his hands to himself may be the one with the sweetest and most helpful spirit; the one who has trouble listening may be the first to

14

share her crayons or loan a pencil to a friend; or the one who gets into trouble on the playground may be the most forgiving and the least judgmental of others. Do we "quietly champion children" who tend to be ostracized? (Gartrell 2001, p. 78).

At first glance, Terry was a student who NEVER did his work, rarely followed along, and always had something better to do. Terry was also not well liked by the other students to the point in which no one wanted to sit by him. I initially was also turned off by Terry's apparent lack of interest and respect for anyone else. Terry and I, however, made our breakthrough in math. I love math and so did Terry. Terry was an exceptional math student and I made sure to let him answer many questions and give examples to the rest of the class. This appeared to get the rest of the class to respect Terry a little more, and in turn, Terry became more involved in the classroom. All I had to do was involve Terry, and Terry transformed into an excellent student who would do nothing but strive to please me. During lessons, I would sit Terry right beside me and let him whisper his answers so that the rest of the class was able to work, uninterrupted. I had to learn from Terry in order for Terry to learn from me (a fifth grade teacher).

Remember, we often need love the most when we're the most unlovable.

ATTENTION

"My teacher is happy to see me every morning." Sometimes, the most precious gift we can give to others is our time and attention – our whole attention. Do you greet each child at the door in the morning? Whether it's a new pair of Asics shoes or a new haircut, take notice. When children tell about an upcoming ball game, recital, or special family event, be sure to ask about it the next day. Josh, a sixth grader, was always clowning around and frustrating his teachers. One spring he earned a very important school sports award. The next day, the teacher was silent; there was no positive affirmation. What a missed opportunity to affirm Josh and build a relationship of trust and respect. Do you know about their siblings, interests, sports, or after school activities? Have lunch with your class once a week. *Be sure to notice all of your children,* even those who are quiet, shy, and compliant; no one should feel invisible or overlooked.

At first, I thought Gabe was nothing more than an average, talkative student. He was constantly talking and never seemed

to be paying attention. When he would complete work, he did exemplary work. I had also noticed that the other students looked up to Gabe and more times than not, followed his example. If the material wasn't important enough for Gabe to pay attention to, why should they? When I took over the classroom, I knew I had to get a better grip on Gabe. Through our mutual love for sports, we started our relationship by simply talking/playing sports on the playground or before or after school. Through that relationship, I gained Gabe's respect. I frequently looked to Gabe to be a leader in my classroom and set a good example for the other students. Gabe became my biggest ally in the classroom. Knowing that everyone, including me, was paying attention to him, Gabe began to complete and turn in all of his work. By the time I left the classroom, Gabe was a member of the Safety Patrol, Honor Roll and boy's basketball team. By gaining Gabe's respect, he respected me and did what he could to please me (fifth grade teacher).

Be sure to give more positive rather than negative attention; avoid nagging and overcorrection. We know that children's need for attention is so strong that if they don't receive what they need when they do things right, they will employ any creative means to *demand* your attention. Harry was loud, obnoxious, and dominating (Rich 1993). He would interrupt others and invade their spaces, yet his negative behavior never reaped enough attention; he was never satisfied. Then Ms. Rich decided to give Harry 10 minutes alone every morning; the principal even arranged for someone to cover her class. Believe it or not, as time went on, his behavior began to improve significantly; he was less hurtful and he exhibited more self-control. Harry desperately needed positive attention and was lucky enough to have a kind and sensitive teacher who gave the greatest gift of all – her time.

An all-day kindergarten teacher rocked one child everyday just to be sure that she gave each child attention. She even recorded their names in her book to be sure she didn't miss anyone.

A word of caution: A fifth grade girl constantly raised her hand for further instructions during seat work. The teacher finally realized that she simply wanted his attention. ("Never do for a child what a child can do for himself," it's called learned helplessness.) So he began to convey confidence in her ability to do the work and delayed his attention until her work was completed.

ACCEPTANCE

All children need to feel accepted - by their peers and by you; they need to belong; they need friends. One of the most difficult life skills is learning how to get along with others. Many employers today are looking for applicants with successful team building and social skills; they need people who can work together. If we aren't intentional now about teaching our children the skills necessary to get along with others, then when will they ever learn?

Whenever I ask teachers where children learn social skills, the answer is always the same – "on the playground." While popular children do engage in positive ways with others, there are many other children who just don't get it. They don't know how to make friends. They try what they know but it never works. They repeat the same inappropriate behaviors over and over because they don't know what else to do. Instead of making friends, they seem to alienate everyone. When do they learn to share, take turns, listen, cooperate, negotiate, compromise, confront with words, follow someone else's suggestion once in awhile, or join a group? Where is the modeling, puppetry, role playing, and the integration of literacy to teach social skills? We have all seen children in upper elementary who were starving for acceptance and yet they were doing all the wrong things. The reason? No one ever taught them how to do it differently!

Catherine, a second grader, came home after a very difficult day with her friends and gave her mom eight rules all teachers should teach all children.

Teachers often tell children to "Use your words" but they never tell them what words to use. Have you ever heard the following child-teacher conversation on a playground, "No one will play with me." "Well, go ask someone to play with you." The problem with that advice is that it doesn't work. Other children simply answer, "No, you can't play." If that same teacher was at a reception, she would not go up to a small group of people and say, "May I enter your conversation?

May I talk with you?" She would simply stand close, listen, and enter in the conversation when appropriate. *We must teach social strategies that work.* Hang back, watch the group, and then join in. What about "Can I help?" or "How do you do that?"

With instruction, peer pairing, modeling, cooperative learning, role playing and positive reinforcement, children can be taught what to say and when to say it. If we do not equip them with practical prosocial skills when they are young, they may never be able to build positive relationships with others as they mature.

> At one such moment, Julie said to her teacher,
> "If I knew them words, I'd have already said 'em!"

AFFECTION

"Touch matters" (Carlson, 2005). We applaud Carlson's review of the research in which she reported that human touch is absolutely

HOW COME YOU SAY YOU LOVE ME BUT YOU NEVER TOUCH ME? ARE YOU SCARED OF MY GERMS OR SOMETHING?

necessary for children's healthy cognitive, physical, and emotional development. What about offering a high five, a hug, or a handshake at the end of the day? Did you know that in almost every Swedish school now, children are encouraged to give shoulder and back massages to one another to reduce classroom stress and foster a caring community? While we strongly endorse the policies and procedures that govern appropriate and respectful touching of children in classrooms (i.e., gentle touches limited to a child's arms, shoulders, head, or back and with the child's permission), we believe the children still need affection. Talk with your principal about the policies for your school.

APPRECIATION

Children need mentors more than they need critics. As teachers, we are models of politeness, patience, courtesy, and helpfulness. It is when children live in an environment that fosters care and concern for one another that they learn kindness, thoughtfulness, and helpfulness.

It is living the Golden Rule, as taught by one wise grandmother, "Do unto others as you would have others do unto you." *We treat our children with the same common courtesies we would extend to our colleagues at work.*

"Thank you."

"I appreciate your help."

Demonstrating appreciation is easy. It's simple and it's contagious, yet it's often the first to be overlooked.

It's you I like.
It's not the things you wear;
It's not the way you do your hair,
But it's you I like.

The way you are right now,
The way down deep inside you.
Not the things that hide you
Not your toys – they're just beside you.

But it's you I like.
Every part of you –
Your skin, your eyes, your feelings
Whether old or new.
I hope that you'll remember
Even when you're feeling blue,
That it's you I like, it's you yourself
It's you. It's you I like.

It's You I Like — © 1973, Fred Rogers

CHAPTER FOUR

"Guidance, as the most subtle art of teaching, depends upon a
well-trained teacher skilled in fruitful observation, that she may
record, advise, and redirect the activities of the children in order
to keep them moving in directions of worth to the child and to
society."

- Patty Smith Hill

OBSERVATION

Children are individuals; they are unique; they are one of a kind.
Therefore, *one of our First Steps of positive child guidance is to determine
who needs what.* Children often lack the vocabulary to tell us how
they feel with words; they have no other option but to act out their
feelings. Their behavior is symptomatic. If children are having difficulty, it is *our* responsibility to translate their behaviors. What are
they trying to tell us? "When caregivers take time to examine the
possible causes of specific unacceptable behaviors, often they are better able to understand why a child behaves in a particular way or acts
out certain behaviors that may or may not be problematic" (Reinsberg, 1999). Even "a good Little League baseball coach will analyze
a pitcher's performance and develop an individual prescription based

on that analysis. Just as all pitchers don't receive the same remedies from high-quality coaches ... neither should all students" (VanSciver, 2003). Teachers call this "individualized instruction," and it applies to child guidance, as well as curriculum. For instance, a refusal to participate in a math lesson may not be disobedience but rather a feeling of insecurity, or a lack of understanding the oral directions, or an inability to understand the lesson. Remember, many children would rather misbehave and suffer the consequences, than be seen as stupid. It is only when we carefully observe children that we can apply specific and individual guidance strategies which will lead to children's successes.

Randy was very slow; it was impossible for him to hurry. His teacher noticed that he stressed easily, especially during transitions. She discovered he was not a procrastinator but a perfectionist! He couldn't stop working until it was exactly right. That's a big difference. Pay close attention. Listen to what they are saying WITH and WITHOUT their words.

Of the whole child

When we observe children, it is important that we look at the whole child – his *cognitive, emotional, social, and physical development*. Each depends on the other; "caring for children doesn't permit separating physical needs from emotional needs" (Brazelton & Greenspan, 2000, p. 177). For example, emotional development affects social connections: If a child feels insecure, rejected, unwanted, and lacks self-esteem, it will be difficult for him to reach out with confidence and make new friends. The physical impacts the social: If a child is not feeling well physically, she will probably be fussy, cranky, and irritable, which makes getting along with others nearly impossible. The cognitive affects the social: It is hard for a child to feel smart when

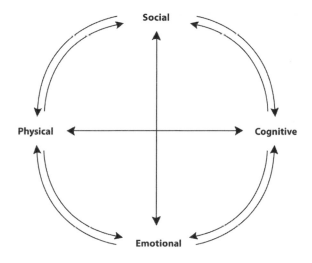

others ridicule or embarrass him. If a child is rejected on the playground in the morning, it will definitely be difficult to concentrate on math in the afternoon.

When children feel physically competent, it promotes self-confidence. (See illustration on the following page.) Take a look, however, at your repertoire of children's games. Many of the traditional playground games alienate children from each other by fostering competition rather than cooperation. "Duck, Duck, Goose" may pass the time but what do children learn? Are we fostering social acceptance, physical competence, and the development of gross motor skills or isolation, rejection, competition, failure, and humiliation? (For alternative games that promote individual skills and team building, please see "Red Rover, Red Rover, It's Time to Move Over" by Staley & Portman, 2000.)

Of personality and temperament

It is also important for teachers to recognize that *a child's personality and temperament will most definitely impact his behavior.* Is he shy, adaptable, inflexible, or moody? When we observe children, do we see how their unique personalities contribute to their positive behaviors or are we trying to make every child into the same square peg so they'll somehow fit into our square holes? What about the children who don't fit into the rigid "everybody sit still and be quiet" expectations?

A particular child was repeatedly told not to talk during passing periods in sixth grade. (If they can't talk in class, can't talk in the lunchroom, and can't talk in the halls, when can they talk?) The teachers were very frustrated and did not appreciate him at all. The student was very social and loved people; he never met anyone he didn't like. When he was no longer there, his friends missed him terribly. "David liked everybody, even the kids nobody else liked. And he always made us laugh during passing periods. School isn't fun anymore without him."

A very social and outgoing child may invade the personal space of others and talk out of turn, but could it be that he just likes people and wants to make them happy? Maybe he is not really trying to cause problems in the classroom; maybe he cares about others and is trying to "de-stress" situations by making people laugh. Maybe he is not striving to be the "center of attention" but just wants his classmates to be happy. These children need "channeling" instead of punishment

(Hymes, 1981, p. 148). Make a list of the characteristics you see in each child. Then think of ways you can channel those qualities in positive ways.

"Many of the most important personality traits, such as the capacities for relating to others, trust and intimacy, empathy, and creative and logical thinking are largely determined by how we nurture a child's nature" (Brazelton & Greenspan, 2000, 82).

DOCUMENTATION

Beginning on the very first day, *record what you see.* Look for patterns in behavior. Does the behavior always occur on the same day of the week? Is it always with the same children? Maybe you are focused on the wrong child. Wolfson-Steinberg (2000) tells a compelling story when she discovered, through very careful observation, that the "obvious instigator," who usually got into trouble, was definitely not the guilty party. It was in fact, the "obvious victim" who was quite manipulative. Her documentation was vital in bringing the truth to light.

Documentation also helps children see what you see. Randy suffered much stress as a kindergartner and cried throughout many of the classroom activities. His kindergarten teacher used documentation to help him see what he was missing. (See illustration on the following page.)

Be sure to record children's positive behaviors, too. One teacher set up a Word document for each child, where she kept a running record of behavior. Another teacher adapted the form on the next page as a color-coded computer template (orange font for negative and blue for positive behaviors). (Note: It is not necessary to complete every line every time. The form is just a prompt to help you recall the event.) Whatever system you choose, documentation is especially

helpful later during family conferences. Parents want to hear specifics about their children and every parent likes to hear good news! Remember, focus on the positive before "failure is locked in" (Brazelton & Greenspan, 2000, 137) because children who experience the most success always seem to succeed, but children who experience the most failure always seem to fail.

OBSERVATION AND DOCUMENTATION OF BEHAVIOR

Date _____ Time _____

Name _____

What happened? _____

What was happening immediately prior to this? _____

_____

Where did it happen? _____

Who was involved? _____

What did you do? _____

Did you contact the family? _____

What was the family response? _____

REFLECTION

Take time to reflect on your observations and documentation. *What are YOU doing? Is it working?* Reflect upon your interaction and relationships with your children. Do you escalate situations by arguing, embarrassing, or humiliating them? Do you back them into a corner, or do give them a way out to protect their dignity? If you are having difficulties during specific times of instruction, reflect on your teaching. Are the children bored? Is the curriculum developmentally appropriate? Are the lessons engaging? If you are having difficulty transitioning, from recess to social studies, observe more carefully and reflect on what you see. If one solution doesn't work, try another and persist until you find the best one. One teacher noticed that her fourth graders always lost control when they turned in their papers and transitioned between subjects. When she created an entirely new organizational strategy for collecting papers and moving to the next subject, order was restored.

Be sure to look at the impact of room arrangement. Does furniture arrangement promote easy movement about the room while minimizing the large and open spaces which suggest running? Are the children visible to you at all times? Does the environment reflect a space owned by the children (e.g. child-designed bulletin boards)? Is the space clearly organized, with low shelving and visual clues, so that children can easily find and replace materials independently? Is the space clutter free and well organized to reduce frustration? Or does your class look like a warehouse with stuff everywhere? If you are not an organizer, find a colleague who is. How about an Extreme Classroom Makeover?

In summary, *observation, documentation, and reflection will reveal your First Steps of positive child guidance.*

(BEFORE)

(AFTER)

CHAPTER FIVE

"A good teacher listens to everybody."
- Catherine, a second grader

COMMUNICATION

If we want to encourage the best behavior in our children, one of the first things we must do is practice effective strategies of communication. We must communicate without judgment, with nonverbal language that matches our words, with positive directions, with clarity, with appropriate choices, without "Why?" and with firmness and calmness. It is totally unfair for us to expect children to behave in positive ways if they do not understand our expectations.

With "I Messages"

"I Messages," as suggested by Thomas Gordon, author of *Parent Effectiveness Training* (1970), have been used as an effective strategy by both teachers and parents for many years. These messages are especially helpful when the adult is frustrated or having a problem with the child's behavior. The format is: "I feel (or "It is not okay") . . . when you . . . because. . . ." For example, "I am disappointed when you don't share your toys because I know you are a kind person." Rather than accusing someone, "I Messages" communicate how one feels. "You Messages" communicate judgment: "You are so selfish; you never share your toys; no wonder no body likes you." "You Messages" prompt defensiveness and resistance; the receiver puts up a wall and communication is closed. "I Messages," however, do not attack the receiver but rather tell how the speaker feels so the receiver is more likely to listen and cooperate.

When adults model effective communication skills, children begin to imitate when resolving conflicts with their peers. "Conflict is a normal part of social development" (Gillespie and Chick, 2001, 192) and an opportunity for teaching and learning. When children are first learning the skills necessary for successful conflict resolution, they are supported by teachers who teach and model effective strategies. We must teach in context. We must seize the teachable moments. We can't wait and teach these skills later in the day. The lessons won't stick!

Teachers sometimes establish a Peace Table or garden bench where children go to mend differences with others. The first rule at the Peace Table is "When one person talks, the other person listens." One teacher created a poster for DEBUG IT: 1) Define the problem, [What happened?] 2) Explain your side of the story, 3) Brainstorm possible solutions together, 4) Use negotiation to find a compromise,

5) Get help, if needed, and 6) Shake on it. When children are first learning these skills, the teacher serves as the mediator. However, Gillespie and Chick (2001) reported much success when they later incorporated peer mediators or "Fussbusters" (p. 192). Olympic View Elementary, Seattle, invites fourth and fifth graders to serve as Conflict Mediators during recess. These students are specially trained to promote dialogue, listen, and negotiate peace; they are very effective.

With positive nonverbal language

Only 7% of what we communicate is through words; an overwhelming 93% is communicated from our tone of voice, inflections, facial expressions, and body language (Zust, 2003). What does your nonverbal language say to your children? When you are all slumped over, do you command respect? When you breathe a heavy sigh, does it say, "I am so-o-o frustrated with you." When you point your finger, does it say, "You never do anything right." On the other hand, do your gentle touches and kind, quiet voices match your words when you say you care? When you are calm in the midst of stress, you communicate control and strength; your children trust you. What do your eyes tell them? *Do you have "shining eyes"* that communicate unconditional love and patience and understanding? Do you have a smile that says, "I like being here with you?" (See illustration on the following page.)

With positive directions

Pretend you are in a restaurant and someone at your table says, "Whatever you do, don't look now, but did you see that over there?" What do you do? You look! Whatever we ask children *not* to do, their brains say *"do it right now."* If we want children to follow directions, tell them in a positive way; tell them what you *want* them to do rather than what you don't want them to do. Say, "When you clear your

desks, we'll go to gym" rather than "If you don't clear your desks, you won't go to gym." Tell them to "Walk, please," instead of "Don't run." The brain simply translates it better.

With clear and specific instructions

"Be good." What does that mean? When we give such ambiguous directions as "Be good," our children have no idea what we expect. Be clear and specific. Tell them exactly what you want them to do. Tell them: "Be quiet." "Keep your hands to yourself." "Sit still." "Listen to directions." "Use walking feet." "Use a quiet voice." It takes almost six weeks for a new class to learn what you want them to do.

It also helps to *avoid, "okay?" at the end of every sentence*. "Okay" implies there is a choice when, in fact, there is no choice. Teacher, "It is time to go inside, okay?" Child, "NO; it is NOT okay; I don't want to go inside!" We do not need to ask permission when giving children directions.

A quick note about counting; observe what happens when you say, "I'm going to count to five and you'd better. . . ." For most children, nothing happens until four, four-and-a-half, four-and-three quarters, etc. What's the point? We believe there is absolutely no need to count. Simply tell children clearly and specifically what you want them to do.

With active listening

Active listening is another technique suggested by Thomas Gordon (1970). It is especially helpful when the *child* is frustrated or having a problem. The teacher tries to understand what the child is communicating and then reflects back that understanding for verification.

Active listening validates a child's feelings and assures him that you understand; it is empathetic. It is not restating or "parroting" what the child says. It is like playing tennis; the child serves the ball by telling you how he feels and you return the serve by reflecting back what you understand. When we give children a chance to vent and talk it out, they often discover a workable solution to their own problems. Many times children don't need a lecture; they just need to be understood.

David was in second grade and had difficulty reading and interacting with others; school was a very stressful and overwhelming environment for him. Quite often during recess, his teacher would rock him and they would talk. "Tell me, what hurts your feelings?" she asked. She showed him she cared by taking special time to listen to his feelings. "I understand," she replied.

Randy, very easily frustrated, was under the table crying hysterically; his kindergarten teacher scooped him up in her lap as she consoled him and they rocked back and forth together on the floor. "I know you hurt inside, honey. Tell me what's wrong. I want to help you. I love you. I care about you."

Remember to listen with your eyes, as well as your ears. *Eye contact says you're really listening.*

With appropriate choices

Children choose how to act; we cannot force them. They choose whether to behave according to our expectations and directions or not. *Our responsibility is to teach them how to make wise choices by experiencing positive consequences for the good decisions and learning from their mistakes.* They must learn to take responsibility for their decisions instead of blaming others. "He made me do it" is not an acceptable response. We must teach children to be accountable for their actions.

If there is a possibility of resistance, we often give children two choices. When children are given reasonable and appropriate choices, within *our* parameters, they gain a sense of control and are often more willing to cooperate; thus, we often avoid unnecessary power struggles. "You may clean up the housekeeping center or the art center." It is only when we give our children the responsibility of making small decisions that they develop the maturity to make bigger decisions later.

Without asking "Why?"

"Why did you hit Billy?" " Because he p----- me off!" What answer did you expect? You'll never get a satisfactory answer to "Why?" Young children's behavior is usually not premeditated; they act before thinking. It is spontaneous. It is triggered by something. Better questions would be: "Tell me what happened." "What were you doing?" "What did you need?" "What did you want?" "Did this help you get what you needed/wanted?" We should be more concerned with knowing what happened, so that the misbehavior is less likely to be repeated and a wiser choice can be made the next time (Wolfson-Steinberg, 2000).

We have also learned to give our immediate attention to the *victim,* rather than the aggressor. *Ask the victim for his/her story first.* (See illustration on the following page.) The aggressor must listen and then answer "What was *right* about that?" Help the children see the problem. Help them see how rules apply. All parties have an opportunity to be heard. When we give our attention to the victim, it demonstrates sympathy and caring. It demonstrates that the injured party is the most important person and deserves your attention first. This sends a very strong, non-verbal message. Try it.

With firmness and calmness

Imagine a young child sneaking out the door into the hall; the teacher says (in a sweet and syrupy voice), "Honey, come back in the room, please." Compare that to the teacher who says (in a strong and deep voice), "Mary, stop right there." Which teacher do you suppose the child will obey? Which teacher sounds serious? It is much more effective to start out the year firm and strong; a teacher can always "loosen up" once the children have learned to respect the teacher's authority, but it is impossible to "tighten up" once children have learned to disregard the teacher.

Being firm does not mean yelling; there is never any need to yell. Yelling and throwing things (i.e., pencils or erasers, etc.) tells everyone the teacher is losing control. It is the quickest way to lose respect

from the children, colleagues, the principal, and families. (You may think no one can see you but your episode will the very first thing your children will tell their families when they get home – GUARANTEED!) A firm, yet calm, tone of voice and assertive body language tells children you're serious and their misbehavior will not be tolerated. You must always, always, always remember to demonstrate self-control and maintain your composure. Losing your temper is *not* an option when working with children. When a child tries to take

control (his will against your will) by manipulating you into a heated argument, STOP. Never fight with a child; you will lose. **Never, never restrain a child or touch a child in anger.** Remember these important words: "Anger is one letter short of Danger" (Josephson, 2005). (See illustration on the preceding page.)

With professionalism

Professionalism is one of the very *First Steps* of positive child guidance. It goes hand in hand with excellence and always striving to be you best. Principals expect it; families expect it; colleagues expect it.

- *Use proper English and correct grammar.*
  - *Never use obscenities, vulgarities, or racial/ethnic/cultural slurs.*
- *Dress appropriately;* casual is fine but sloppiness is not.
  - When you dress sloppy, you teach sloppy!
    (Sloppiness says, "I don't deserve respect.")
    (Sloppiness says "I don't respect my class enough to take the time to look professional.")
    (Sloppiness says to children , "You aren't worth it.")
  - Avoid cotton sweat shirts and sweat pants.
  - Avoid flip flops.
  - *Be modest:* no exposed tummy; no drooping pants; no cleavage; and no mini skirts.
- *Teach as if you were Teacher of the Year, because for your class you are!*
- *Establish loving leadership.* You are the teacher; your goal is not to be their best friend; your goal is to teach. If you are an excellent teacher, they will love you.

CHAPTER SIX

"Treat others as you would like to be treated."

- a wise grandmother

CONSISTENCY

Consistency is the second foundational philosophy of positive child guidance. Our level of tolerance is not dependent on what mood we are in, how we feel, or how much sleep we had the night before. We are enthusiastic, energetic, and cheerful on Fridays but irritable, lethargic, and cranky on Mondays. We don't ignore minor misbehaviors with some children but nag others. Our expectations are consistent. For instance, our rules for today should be the same rules tomorrow. In this chapter, we will talk about planning for transitions, maintaining reasonable expectations, making our "NO" mean "NO," teaching children to listen, picking our battles, using logical consequences, and giving consistent feedback. Believe it or not, children are sincerely trying to please us, but it is very difficult to do that if our expectations and standards for their behavior keep changing. If they eventually determine that they can never please us, they will give up and quit trying, and that is the very worst thing that can happen.

By planning for transitions

It helps to give children a five minute warning *before* transitions. If children are still finishing seat work, a five minute warning lets them know that closure is coming. Imagine sitting at your computer typing a long e-mail to a friend and the computer shuts down. You've lost the letter that took you 15 minutes to write! If only a warning signal had sounded and an alert message flashed across the screen telling you that you had five minutes to save your document before shut down. Children need the same thing. They need to prepare for upcoming transitions.

Effective teachers plan for transitions with the same intentionality

as literacy and numeracy. They know that chaos develops when teachers leave transitions to chance. If one transition strategy doesn't work, try another. Think of transitions as the bridges that connect your curriculum (Moss, 1997/1998). Be prepared. Have materials ready. Unnecessary waiting time is a catalyst for confusion and conflict. Allow enough time. When children are rushed, they feel stressed. "Hurry up! Hurry up!" breeds tension for everybody. Take the extra time, during the first few weeks of school, to teach the children how you want them to conclude their lesson, put things away, line up, and transition to Specials (library, gym, music, art, etc.) smoothly and on time. This takes practice.

By maintaining developmentally appropriate rules and expectations
Design classroom rules or "codes of conduct" (Albert, L. cited in Charles, 2005, p. 215), keeping in mind that any rule should be *reasonable, age appropriate and protect the safety of all children.* (DeVries and Zan, 2003). Only make rules you are willing to enforce with all of the children all of the time. Post the rules so they are easily visible, and teach them systematically and intentionally. Always teach in context. For instance, when children have difficulty learning how to transition quickly and smoothly, plan ahead to allow the extra time necessary to stop and practice right then. Seize the teachable moment. Frequent and consistent reinforcement of the rules during the beginning of school will help children establish year long habits of positive behavior.

Some sample rules are: *1) Be gentle with your actions; 2) Be kind with your words;* and *3) Be helpful in our school.* One kindergarten teacher has *"High 5 Rules:" 1) Willing hearts, 2) Good attitudes, 3) Turned on minds, 4) Listening ears,* and *5) Looking eyes.* Another kindergarten teacher has the following rules: (She calls her children

51

"Smarties" because they are her "smartest" children.) *1) Smarties listen to others; 2) Smarties treat others with kindness; 3) Smarties take care of our school* (i.e., "In the restroom, put the trash in the wastebasket and not on the floor;" "Keep your hands off the hallway walls."); *4) Smarties treat others with kindness* (i.e., "You may not like someone but they deserve your respect. You don't have to play ball together on the playground but you have to learn together in the classroom."); and *5) When I talk, you listen.*

In the beginning of the year, expect your children to test the rules; be patient and persevere; consistency will be your key to success. It takes three to six weeks for children to learn how to behave in *your* classroom. The younger the class, the longer it takes. (For further consideration of rules, see *From Policing to Participation: Overturning*

the Rules and Creating Amiable Classrooms by Wien, 2004 and *Rules in School* by Brady, Forton, Porter, and Wood, 2003.)

By making "NO" mean "NO"

"NO" means "NO." "NO" does not mean "Maybe" or "Ask me later and I will change my mind." "NO" means "NO." When "NO" frequently changes to "YES," do you know what children learn to do? They learn to argue. If they argue long enough, the teacher will change his mind. Don't play the Arguing Game; it will never end and you will lose. *Say what you mean and mean what you say.* Think before you give your answer. A fifth grade teacher introduced a new spelling game. The instructions were clear: If the class does not maintain control, the game will stop. Day 1: Shortly after the game started, the

children lost control. He said, "No more" and stopped the game; the children began to argue but the teacher simply went on to the next lesson. Day 2: The game lasted about 5 minutes. Day 5: the children enjoyed the game within the parameters established by the teacher. The class learned that when the teacher said "NO," he meant "NO."

By teaching children to listen

Get their attention first. Have an attention signal. Ring a bell or clap. (Teacher claps: clap-clap, clapclapclap. Children respond and repeat: clap-clap, clapclapclap.) Make eye contact. Avoid repeating yourself. When we continue to repeat our instructions, children learn *not* to listen the first time. One teacher noticed the children had tuned her out and were not listening to her directions, so she stopped in mid-sentence. She caught the attention of a few. She continued and stopped again in mid-sentence. Pretty soon, they all knew she expected them to listen. Try it. It works.

By *picking our battles*

While always protecting children's safety, *it is wise to ignore minor misbehaviors.* So many times we engage in needless struggles over insignificant issues rather than "picking our battles." We need to prioritize and focus on the most important behavioral issues first, such as those related to safety. "My job is to keep everyone safe. I won't let you hurt anyone here, but I won't let anyone hurt you either." A wise professor and long time kindergarten teacher once told us that she used to decide whether or not to address a particular behavior by asking the question, "Is this a long-term issue? Will this affect his life?" (Williams, 1992). If not, perhaps it isn't necessary to make a big deal out of it right now and go on to the more important issues.

One teacher informed a parent that she was moving Bill's desk next to hers to help him focus. The parent refused and yelled, "I will not have him isolated. You are harassing him, and I will call the authorities!" The teacher dropped the issue; it wasn't worth it. A few weeks later, the mother called and said, "Our counselor helped me see what you see. I understand now. You may move Bill's desk."

When we give a child the support he needs to be successful in one important thing (i.e. playing safe with others on the playground), he senses "I can do this!" and then he is ready to tackle the next issue. We don't try to correct all of his problems all at once. When we pick on everything a child does wrong, he quickly becomes frustrated, stops listening and gives up; the battle is over and everyone loses. We must give consistent attention on the "majors" and less attention on the "minors;" that is the key to "picking our battles." Author Richard Carlson (1997) says it best, "Don't Sweat the Small Stuff…and it's all small stuff."

A fourth grade boy liked to spit. This really irritated his teacher; she though it was gross and unnecessary. She tried everything and could not get him to quit spitting. Finally, she gave up and said, "You can spit in the grass but don't let me see it." It worked. Everyone was happy. He could spit in the grass but she didn't have to watch.

By using natural and logical consequences

Punishment is usually arbitrary, unreasonable, inappropriate, unrelated, delayed, and unexpected. It usually breeds resentment and rebellion, as well as stress, frustration and confusion for children. Logical consequences, however, are constructive, reasonable, appropriate, connected and immediate. We want to look for solutions that teach. When a child makes a mess, she cleans it up. When a child marks on a desk, he scrubs it off. *Logical consequences make sense and teach at the same time.*

Understanding that each child is unique, we need to look for consequences that motivate change — consequences that "trip their triggers." Keep in mind that what motivates one child may not motivate another. Barbara Coloroso (1994) suggested that when deciding on appropriate consequences, we should think RSVP: Is it reasonable

and logical? Is it simple? Is it valuable teaching? Is it practical? She also suggested that effective consequences should address Restitution (repair or replacement), Resolution (won't happen again), and Reconciliation (healing relationships).

By giving consistent feedback

We cannot give negative feedback to one child but ignore the same misbehaviors in other children. The children who irritate the most and "get under your skin" are the very ones who are usually "nailed" for every little thing. Be careful. We must be consistent with all children, with both our negative and positive feedback. *Children respond much better to our disapproval when it is coupled with the fre-*

quent acknowledgment of the many things they do right. When you are trying to teach a child to raise his hand, instead of talking out, try praising him when he does it right. The more he is successful, the more he will learn to raise his hand. Notes home and other positive reinforcements are wonderful opportunities to let children know their strengths. (Positive messages also help parents affirm children's wonderful qualities, too.)

"If you punish one kid, then be sure to punish the other kid, too, if they were doing the same thing, or the one punished will NEVER forget that you weren't fair." (sixth grader)

CHAPTER SEVEN

"The child will have an imprint of his culture upon him."

\- Margaret Mead

The Bigger Picture
In the context of families

Children live within the context of their homes, neighborhoods, and communities. They are raised in environments that reflect cultural and religious values, attitudes, and behaviors (Bronfenbrenner, 1970). Family structures differ. Home languages differ. We must be diversity literate (Derman-Sparks & the ABC Task Force, 1989) if we are to develop family relationships that communicate our sincerity and foster trust and respect. Only then can we build effective partnerships with families. We have a responsibility to equip, empower, and enable each family in their role as their child's first teacher. We send home a Welcome Letter on the first day of school. We call each parent during the first week of school to let them know we notice something special and wonderful about their child. On Orientation Night, we welcome families and share our curriculum goals and strategies for positive child guidance. With the children's assistance, we publish a monthly classroom newsletter. When we have family conferences, we share our documentation and seek to learn from each another

Family stresses also differ. The family could be coping with an aging grandparent, a serious illness, hospitalization, a new baby, a recent divorce and/or remarriage, military service, or death of a family member. Many of our children are living personal lives of silent abandonment, neglect, rejection, hunger, and abusive horrors.

The sixth grader's mom was an alcoholic. His father died earlier that year. On good nights, Grandma gave him a little money so he could walk eight blocks to the local Village Pantry to buy dinner. He did his own homework. He put himself to bed and he woke himself up in the morning. His bedroom was added to the back of the house with no heat in the Midwest winters. He couldn't participate in any after-school activities because he had to ride the bus home; there was no one to pick him up if he missed the bus. He was bussed from the inner city to the suburbs, which was at least four miles away.

No discussion of child guidance can take place without our sensitivity to the context in which our children live. Observe them closely. Have you noticed a change in a child's behavior? Is he more tired, cranky, irritable or volatile? Punishment is not what he needs; he needs your intervention. *Listen to what children are saying with and without their words. Listen well with your eyes to what they are tying to tell you and listen with your heart to what they hope you will hear.*

In the context of health and wellness: sleep, diet, and play

The behaviors of children who are chronically sleep deprived are quite similar to the behaviors of children with Attention Deficit Disorder (Kantrowitz & Springen, 2003). Young children need between ten and twelve hours of sleep per night. The lack of sleep affects not only health but also mood and the ability to learn. If children are getting up at 6:30, they need to be in bed no later than 8:30, if they are to get the minimum of ten hours of sleep. Children don't know when they are sleepy. To facilitate a good night's sleep for our children, it is helpful to encourage families to establish a bedtime routine to reduce the bedtime battles. The body will then begin to respond to the bath, teeth brushing, pajamas, story time, and music by winding down and starting to feel sleepy.

Diet also affects behavior. Diets high in sugar, caffeine, chemicals, preservatives, and food dyes often have a negative impact on children's behavior. *Excessive fidgeting, difficulty concentrating, and impulsivity may also be linked to food allergies* (Atkinson, 2005). Atkinson reviewed twenty-five years of research related to the "food-mood" connection.

- A balanced breakfast of proteins and complex carbohydrates promoted self-control and attention, while skipping breakfast triggered irritability and fatigue.
- Most children also need a mid-morning snack to stabilize their blood sugar and improve their ability to concentrate. A drop in blood sugar by late morning or too much sugar later in the day may trigger anger.
- Deficiencies in protein, iron, zinc, and B vitamins at age three were related to hyperactivity and aggression in later years.
- Some children who exhibited hyperactivity also had low levels of calcium.
- Three studies reported that up to 60% of children with ADHD suffered from increased misbehaviors after ingesting chemical dyes and preservatives.
- Eggs, milk, bananas, chicken and turkey tend to be calming foods, which offset anxiety and/or depression. It was reported that tuna and salmon were related to increased attention, learning, and memory for children with ADHD.

Barbara Stitt, a former chief probation officer and author of *Food and Behavior* and *Roadmap to Healthy Foods in Schools* reported much success when she instituted a low sugar diet for convicts. Her work was the basis of the documentary *Super Size Me*. She states unequivocally that "Junk food abuses the mind, undernourishes the body, and distorts behavior'" (Cited in Atkinson, 2005, p. 21). Schools in Wisconsin and Illinois have reported major changes in children's behaviors simply by removing junk food vending machines and reconstructing school lunch menus. Perhaps one of our first steps in helping children to behave in positive ways is to survey their food intake.

Children also need unstructured time to play. Do your children have regularly scheduled time-outside or has recess been cancelled? Be their advocate for play. The children who usually lose recess privileges are the very ones who need outside play the most. The American Association for the Child's Right to Play (www.IPA/USA.org) and the Association for Childhood Education International's (www.acei. org) joint position statement, *Play: Essential for All Children*, is an excellent resource for further information and advocacy for children's time for play. Note: soccer, swimming, music lessons and scouts are all fine, as long as every hour of every day is not filled with scheduled activities. *We must encourage families to set aside time for unstructured play.*

CHAPTER EIGHT

"Schools must do what they can to contribute to the character of
the young and the moral health of a nation."

- Thomas Lickona

A Caring Community
Within the classroom

A caring community is built upon trust and respect. Children trust
the teacher to be all that he/she teaches them to be; it's called integ-
rity. It's about living what we teach and living what we believe. As we
model respect, we emphasize the similarities and differences in our
children (Derman-Sparks and the ABC Task Force, 1989). When
our children learn to see through the eyes of another, they begin to
understand someone else's point of view; they develop empathy and
compassion.

If we were to sum up all that we believe about promoting positive
child guidance, it would be to create a caring community within each
classroom where each child is responsible to the community and the

community is responsive to each child – a connected family. A family looks for ways to help each other. A family protects each other. A family trusts each other. A family cares about each other and respects each other.

Do your children feel mutually appreciated (Gartrell, 2001)? To foster a sense of community, many teachers incorporate daily class meetings where children are empowered to be respectful problem solvers, as they bring concerns, conflicts, and challenges before the group for consideration and discussion. The children are taken seriously. "We don't have to come up with solutions. In fact, sometimes it may be better if we don't. The fact that an issue has been discussed – articulated by the child concerned and heard by all – is perhaps the most important part of the process" (McClurg, 1998, 33). Class meetings promote reconciliation and resolution when children are taught that friends respect each other by a) giving everyone a chance to speak, b) listening, c) letting others finish (do not interrupt), d) acknowledging the feelings of others, and e) working together for a solution.

The Responsive Classroom (www.responsiveclassroom.org) is an excellent resource to assist teachers with specific suggestions and strategies for developing a caring community (i.e., rules, morning meetings, classroom spaces, and friendships). Bondy and Ketts (2001) incorporate Morning Meetings as a time for sharing, acceptance, planning, and transition. For this, a teacher might use the following promts: a) "What would you like us to know about you?" b) "If you are feeling angry or sad today, how can we support you?" and c) "If you are happy or excited about something, tell us so we can be happy with you. One student said, "You get to know each other in Morning Meetings. You learn to get along with each other and you get to know each other's lives. So if someone feels bad, you know that person and you could help them" (p. 147).

"The Six Pillars of Character," sponsored by Character Counts (Josephson, 2006) also contributes to a caring community. It is another resource which emphasizes the virtues of trustworthiness, respect, responsibility, fairness, caring, and citizenship. Children learn *Trustworthiness* by telling the truth, doing what they say they'll do, and keeping their promises. Children learn *Respect* by being courteous and considerate, following the Golden Rule, accepting differences, and being peacemakers. Children learn *Responsibility* by doing their best, using self-control and self-discipline, thinking before they act, and being accountable for their choices. Children learn *Fairness* by taking turns, sharing, listening to others, and not blaming others carelessly or falsely. Children learn *Caring* by being kind, compassionate, forgiving, and helpful. Children learn *Citizenship* when they cooperate, obey the rules, respect authority, and protect the environment. Many materials are available at www.charactercounts.org to promote the instruction, positive reinforcement, and modeling of these core

values with children of all ages.

To further create a caring community, Daniel Gartrell (2001) suggests that children learn "democratic life skills: a) to see one's self as a worthy individual and a capable member of the group, b) to express strong emotions in non-hurting ways, c) to solve problems ethically and intelligently, d) to be understanding of the feelings and viewpoints of others, and e) to work cooperatively in groups, with acceptance of the human differences among members" (Gartrell, 1988, and cited in Gartrell, 2001, p. 76- 77). (See illustration on the previous page.)

Ultimately, a caring community is about shared support of one another. It is emotionally and physically safe. (See illustration on the following page.) There is a lack of tension and an absence of competition. There is laughter, friendliness, and cheerfulness.

Within the school

As you think about developing a caring community in your classroom, it is also helpful to develop a support system within your teaching team. For instance, identify your own strengths and weaknesses. Be open-minded. If you are creative but unorganized, share your creativity and seek help with your clutter.

You may also work together on behalf of your children. For instance, one kindergartner who had difficulties managing his stress was taught to tell the teacher, "I need out," at which time the teacher would call the school psychologist and say, "Randy needs you." The psychologist would take Randy to her office for some art therapy or bibliotherapy or whatever Randy needed at that time. The intervention was so effective in kindergarten that the first and second grade teachers continued to use the same strategy with Randy. That is a caring community!

Our Best Advice

Attitude is everything — so choose a good one. Do you look forward to walking into your class every day? Do you love what you do? Does it show?

A favorite first grade teacher always has the most cheerful and most cooperative children in the building. Why? Because she is always cheerful, whether she feels like it or not. Whether her husband has just been deployed to Iraq, her daughter has gone off to college, or she was up late with her son's ball game, she knows she is "on stage"

- CATHERINE, A SECOND GRADER, CAME HOME AFTER SCHOOL TO TELL HER MOM ABOUT HER DAY. -

OH MOM, IT WAS AN AWFUL DAY FOR MY FRIEND SARAH. SHE WAS REAL SAD BECAUSE HER GRANDPA DIED LAST NIGHT, AND THEN THE TEACHER WOULDN T LET HER BE THE LINE LEADER, AND THEN HER BEST FRIENDS WOULDN T PLAY WITH HER ON THE PLAYGROUND. SO WE SAT ON THE STEPS AND I GAVE HER A HUG, AND SHE CRIED ON MY SHOULDER.

the moment she walks into her school every morning. The spotlight is on her. The children simply imitate and reflect her cheerfulness. As children continue to "grow out" of her class, they always go back to visit their favorite teacher.

Attitudes are contagious; is yours worth catching?

Have a sense of humor! Laugh out loud! Chill out! Relax! Lighten Up!

OUR BEST ADVICE:

Enjoy your children. Enjoy every single one.

REFERENCES

Atkinson, W. (2005). Food mood: Feeding problem behaviors. *Children's Voice,* 14 (4): 18-21.

Bakley, S. (1997). Love a little more, accept a little more. *Young Children,* 52(2): 21.

Bondy, R. & Ketts, S. (2001). "Like being at the breakfast table: The power of classroom morning meeting." *Childhood Education,* 77(3): 144-149.

Boss, B. (1992). When I say something about a kid and I know it's right, I don't compromise. *Dimensions,* 20(2): 11.

Brady, K., Forton, M., Porter, D., & Wood, C. (2003). *Rules in school.* Greenfield, MA: The Northeast Foundation for Children.

Brazelton, T. B. & Greenspan, S.I. (2000). *The irreducible needs of children: What every child must have to grow, learn, and flourish.* Cambridge, MA: Perseus.

Bredekamp, S. & Copple, C. eds. (1997). *Developmentally appropriate practice in early childhood programs.* Washington, DC: National Association for the Education of Young Children (NAEYC).

Bronfenbrenner, U. (1970). *Two worlds of childhood: US and USSR.* NY: Russell.

Carlson, F. (2005). Significance of touch in young children's lives. *Young Children,* 60(4): 79-85.

Carlson, R. (1997*). Don't sweat the small stuff. . . and it's all small stuff: Simple ways to keep the little things from taking over your life.* NY: Hyperion.

Castle, K. (2004). *The meaning of autonomy in early childhood teacher education. Journal of Early Childhood Teacher Education,* 25: 3-10.

Charles, C. with Senter, G. (2005). *Building classroom discipline.* Boston, MA: Pearson.

Copple, C. & Bredekamp, S. (2006). *Basics of developmentally appropriate practice.* Washington, DC: (NAEYC).

Coloroso, B. (1994). *Kids are worth it.* NY: Harper Collins.

Derman-Sparks, L & the ABC Task Force. (1989). *Anti-bias*

curriculum: Tools for empowering young children. Washington,
DC: NAEYC.

DeVries, R. & Zan, B. (2003). *When children make rules. Educational Leadership,* 61(1): 64-67.

Gartrell, D. (2006). Guidance matters. *Young Children,* 61(2): 88-89.

Gartrell, D. (2001). Replacing time-out: Part One – Using guidance to build an encouraging classroom. *Young Children,* 56(6): 72-78.

Gillespie, C. W. & Chick, A. (2001). Fussbusters: Using peers to mediate conflict resolution in a Head Start classroom. *Childhood Education,* 77(4):192-195.

Gordon, T. (1970). *Parent effectiveness training: The No-Lose program for raising responsible children.* NY: Peter Wyden, Inc.

Humphrey, S. (1989). The case of myself. *Young Children,* November: 17-22.

Hymes, J. (1981). *Teaching the child under six.* Merrill: Columbus, OH.

Josephson Institute of Ethics (2006). *Character Counts.* www.charactercounts.org.

Josephson Institute of Ethics (2005). *Character Counts.* Poster series.

Kantrowitz, B. & Springen, K. (2003). September 22. Why sleep matters. *Newsweek*, 75.

Katz, L. (1999). Personal conversation.

McClurg, L. G. (1998). Building an ethical community in the classroom community meeting. *Young Children*, 53(2): 30-35.

Merriam-Webster. (1989). *Webster's Ninth Collegiate Dictionary*. Springfield, MA: Author.

Moss, J. (1997/1998). Helping student teachers improve transitions in the classroom: Are we as teacher educators part of the problem? *Childhood Education*, 74(2): 96F & N.

NAEYC. (2006). *NAEYC develops 10 standards of high-quality early childhood education*. www.naeyc.org/about/releases/20060416.asp.

Olympic View Elementary School. www.seattleschools.org/schools/ olyview/activities.htm. Retrieved on 6/20/09.

Readdick, C. & Chapman, P. (2000). Young children's perception of time-out. *Journal of Research in Childhood Education*, 15(1): 81-87.

Reinsberg, M. (1999). Understanding young children's behavior. *Young Children*, 54(4): 54-57.

Rich, B. A. (1993). Listening to Harry (And solving a problem in my kindergarten classroom!) *Young Children*, 48(6): 52-53.

Scarmadella, T. & Daggett, S. (1997). Teacher to teacher. *The Responsive Classroom*, 9(1): 8-9.

Simon, S. (1991). *I am lovable and capable: A modern allegory on the classical put-down*. Hadley, MA: Values Press.

Smith-Hill, P. (1992). Kindergarten. *American Educator Encyclopedia*, 1971.

Staley, L. & Portman, P.A. (2000). "Red Rover, Red Rover, It's time to move over!" *Young Children*, 55(1): 67-70.

VanSciver, J. (2003). Motherhood, apple pie, and differentiated instruction. *Phi Delta Kappan*, 86(7): 534-535.

Wein, C. A. (2004). From policing to participation: Overturning the rules and creating amiable classrooms. *Young Children*, 59(1).

Williams, A. (1991). Personal conversation.

Wolfson-Steinberg, L. (2000). "Teacher! He hit me!" "She pushed me!" – Where does it start? How can it stop? *Young Children*, 55(3): 38-42.

Zust, C. W. (2003). *The power of nonverbal language*. www.zustco.com.

ADDITIONAL
RESOURCES

Adams, S.K. & Baronberg, J. (2005). *Promoting positive behavior: Guidance strategies for early childhood settings.* Upper Saddle River, NJ: Pearson Merrill Prentice Hall.

Bailey, B.A. (2000). *Conscious discipline: 7 basic skills for brain smart classroom management.* Oviedo, FL: Loving Guidance, Inc.

Bailey, B.A. (2002). *Easy to love, difficult to discipline.* New York: Quill Harper Collins Publisher, Inc.

Bailey, B. A. (2003). *There's got to be a better way: Discipline that works for parents & teachers.* Oviedo: FL: Loving Guidance, Inc.

77

Beaty, J.J. (1995). *Converting conflicts in preschool.* Orlando, FL: Harcourt Brace & Company.

Beaty, J.J. (1999). *Prosocial guidance for the preschool child.* Upper Saddle River, NJ: Prentice Hall.

Brady, K., Forton, M.B., Porter, D. & Wood, C. (2003). *Rules in School.* Greenfield, MA: Northeast Foundation for Children.

Charney, R. S. (2000). *Teaching children to care: Management in the responsive classroom.* Greenfield, MA: Northeast Foundation for Children.

Cherry, C. (1983). *Please don't sit on the kids: Alternatives to punitive discipline.* Belmont, CA: David S. Lake Publishers.

Charles, C.M. & Senter, G.W. (2005). *Building Classroom Discipline.* Boston: Pearson: Allyn and Bacon.

Crary, E. (1979). *Without spanking or spoiling: A practical approach to toddler and preschool guidance.* Seattle, WA: Parenting Press.

Daleo, M.S. (1996). *Curriculum of love: Cultivating the spiritual nature of children.* Charlottesville, VA: Grace Publishing & Communications.

ERIC Development Team. (1990). *Positive discipline.* (ERIC Document Reproduction Service No. ED327271).

Essa, E. (1995). *A practical guide to solving preschool behavior problems*. Albany, NY: Delmar Publishers.

Feldman, J. (1995*). Transition time: Let's do something different!*. Beltsville, MD: Gryphon House.

Fields, M.V. & Boesser, C. (2002*). Constructive guidance and discipline: Preschool and primary education*. Upper Saddle River, NJ: Merrill Prentice Hall.

Fields, M. & Fields, D. (2006). *Constructive guidance and discipline: Preschool and primary education*. Upper Saddle River, NJ: Pearson Prentice Hall.

Gartrell, D. (2003). *A guidance approach for the encouraging classroom*. Canada: Thomson Learning.

Gartrell, D. (2004). *The power of guidance: Teaching social-emotional skills in early childhood classrooms*. Canada: Thomson Learning.

Gilstrap, R. & Sunderlin, S. (Eds.). (1981). *Toward self-discipline: A guide for parents and educators*. Washington, DC: Association for Childhood Education International.

Harlan, J.C. (1996). *Behavior management strategies for teachers: Achieving instructional effectiveness, student success, and student motivation-every teacher and any student can!* Springfield, IL: Charles C. Thomas Publisher.

Hearron, P.F. & Hildebrand, V. (2005). *Guiding Young Children*. Upper Saddle River, NJ: Pearson Merrill Prentice Hall.

Hildebrand, V. (1994). *Guiding young children.* New York: Macmillan College Publishing Company.

Marion, M. (2003*). Guidance of young children.* Upper Saddle River, NJ: Merrill Prentice Hall.

Miller, D.F. (2004). *Positive child guidance.* Canada: Thomson Delmar Learning.

Reynolds, E. (1996). *Guiding young children: A child-centered approach.* Mountain View, CA: Mayfield Publishing Company.

Rich, B.A. (1993). Listening to Harry (And solving a problem in my kindergarten classroom!). *Young Children,* 48(6), p. 52-53.

Smith, C.A. (1993). *The peaceful classroom.* Beltsville, MD: Gryphon House.

Stone, J. G. (1989). *A guide to discipline.* Washington DC: National Association for the Education of Young Children.

Tauber, R. T. (1995). *Classroom management: Theory and practice.* Orlando, FL: Harcourt Brace College Publishers.

Vance, E. & Weaver, P.J. (2002). *Class meetings: Young children solving problems together.* Washington DC: National Association for the Education of Young Children.

Wheeler, E.J. (2004). *Conflict resolution in early childhood: Helping children understand and resolve conflicts.* Upper Saddle River, NJ:

Pearson Merrill Prentice Hall.

Wolfgang, C.H. (1995). *Solving discipline problems: Methods and models for today's teachers.* Boston: Allyn & Bacon.

Wolfgang, C.H. & Wolfgang, M.E. (1995*). The three faces of discipline for early childhood: Empowering teachers and students.* Boston: Allyn & Bacon.

CHILDREN'S
LITERATURE LIST

Bang, M. (1999). *When Sophie gets angry-Really, really angry.* New York: Scholastic, Inc.

Beaumont, K. (2004). *I like myself! I'm glad I'm me.* New York: Scholastic, Inc.

Burnett, K.G. (2001). *Katie's rose: A tale of two late bloomers.* Roseville, CA: GR Publishing.

Cain, J. (2000). *The way I feel.* New York: Scholastic, Inc.

Carlson, N. (1988). *I like me!* New York: Penquin Books USA, Inc.

Carlson, N. (2001). *How about a hug?* New York: Scholastic, Inc.

Chardiet, B. & Maccarone, G. (1990). *The playground bully.* New York: Scholastic, Inc.

Charles, F. & Terry, M. (2000). *The selfish crocodile.* New York: Scholastic, Inc.

Couric, K. (2000). *The brand new kid.* New York: Random House, Inc.

Curtis, J. L. (1998). *Today I feel silly and other moods that make my day.* New York: Scholastic, Inc.

Curtis, J.L. & Cornell, L. (2002). *I'm gonna like me.* Harper Collins Publishers.

Dorfman, C. (2003). *I knew you could! A book for all the stops in your life.* New York: Scholastic, Inc.

Emmett, J. & Harry, R. (2003). *Ruby in her own time.* New York: Scholastic, Inc.

Galloway, R. (2001). *Fidgety fish.* New York: Scholastic, Inc.

Ginsburg, M. (1976). *Two greedy bears.* New York: Aladdin Books.

Hazen, B.S. (1981). *Even if I did something awful.* New York: Aladdin Paperbacks.

Henkes, K. (2000). *Wemberly worried.* New York: Scholastic, Inc.

Joosse, B. M. (1998). *I love you the purplest.* New York: Scholastic, Inc.

Kaiser, C. (2004). *If you're angry and you know it!* New York: Scholastic, Inc.

Kraus, R. (1971). *Leo the late bloomer.* New York: Simon Schuster, Inc.

Lester, H. (1994). *It wasn't my fault.* New York: Scholastic, Inc.

Lipkind, W. & Mordvinoff, N. (1951). *Finders keepers.* Orlando, FL: Harcourt Brace Jovanovich Publishers.

Modesitt, J. (1992). *Sometimes I feel like a mouse.* New York: Scholastic, Inc.

O'Neill, A., & Huliska-Beith, L. (2002). *The recess queen.* New York: Scholastic, Inc.

Pfister, M. (2002). *Just the way you are.* New York: Scholastic, Inc.

Scholes, K. (1989). *Peace begins with you.* San Francisco: Sierra Club Books.

Spelman, C.M. (2000). *When I feel angry.* New York: Scholastic, Inc.

Spelman, C.M. (2003). *When I feel good about myself.* New York:

Scholastic, Inc.

Thomas, P. (2000). *Stop picking on me*. New York: Scholastic, Inc.

Viorist, J. (1972). *Alexander and the terrible, horrible, no good, very bad day*. New York: Scholastic, Inc.

Wells, R. (1973). *Noisy Nora*. New York: Scholastic, Inc.

Wood, A. (1982). *Quick as a cricket*. Singapore: Child's Play (International) Ltd.

About the Author

Lynn Staley, Ed.D. is a Professor of Early Childhood Education in the department of Elementary Education at Ball State University (BSU), Muncie, IN. She taught public and private kindergarten for ten years and served as the director of Park Place Church of God Children's Center in Anderson, IN for five years.

Dr. Staley is particularly interested in issues related to international advocacy for children and families. Her current multi-media teacher education project, in conjunction with the Association for Childhood Education International, fosters *Education for Global Citizenship* in the elementary classroom.

As a representative of the Association for Childhood Education International (ACEI), Dr. Staley held consultative status with the United Nations, UNESCO, and UNICEF from 2002-2006 and served as chair of UNICEF's NGO Working Group on Education.

Dr. Staley was also invited by UNICEF to attend the Consultative Group on Early Childhood Care and Development (CGECCD), UNESCO headquarters in Paris (2005), as a representative of ACEI and the Organization Mondiale pour l'Education Prescolaire (OMEP). Approximately 52 early childhood scholars and other advocates were invited from nearly every region of the world.

Dr. Staley was also invited to attend the 1st *Special Session on Children*, sponsored by the United Nations General Assembly (2002).

As an invitee to the Zurich Symposium (1999), sponsored by ACEI and OMEP, Staley was a contributing author for a landmark document outlining international criteria for quality early childhood programming. It is the only early childhood education program assessment tool available today that was originally designed for international use by an international consortium of early childhood scholars and advocates. In 2002, this document was used as the foundation for the *ACEI Global Guidelines Self-Assessment Tool*, which is now published in over seven languages and can be found at www.acei.org.

Dr. Staley has studied early childhood programs in Reggio Emilia, Italy, and visited the International Montessori Center in Perugia, Italy. She has taken undergraduate and graduate students to study abroad in Worcester, England, and Soissons, France.

She has earned the Who's Who Among America's Teachers award (2005), the Outstanding Service Award from BSU Teachers College (2004), the Certificate of Special United States Congressional Recognition (2002), and the Outstanding Teaching Award from BSU Teachers College (2001).

A full list of Staley's publications and presentations is available at www.bsu.edu/elementaryeducation.

About The First Steps Library

The First Steps Library is a series designed for busy people. The books are short and succinct. Additional resources are always available if the reader wants to delve further into a particular topic. Upcoming books in the series can be viewed at www.firststepslibrary.com.

NOTES

NOTES

NOTES

NOTES

NOTES

NOTES

NOTES

Notes

NOTES

NOTES